INJURY

poems by

Maggie Hellwig

Finishing Line Press
Georgetown, Kentucky

INJURY

Copyright © 2021 by Maggie Hellwig
ISBN 978-1-64662-614-4 First Edition
All rights reserved under International and Pan-American Copyright Conventions. No part of this book may be reproduced in any manner whatsoever without written permission from the publisher, except in the case of brief quotations embodied in critical articles and reviews.

ACKNOWLEDGMENTS

I would like to thank the anonymous participants and the support of my friends at School of the Art Institute of Chicago.

Publisher: Leah Huete de Maines

Editor: Christen Kincaid

Cover Art: Anna Goraczko, "Dirt & Hands," cyanotype on cotton, 8.5" x 11", 2020

Author Photo: Maggie Hellwig

Interior Photos: Photos submitted to author anonymously and Maggie Hellwig

Cover Design: Elizabeth Maines McCleavy

Order online: www.finishinglinepress.com
also available on amazon.com

Author inquiries and mail orders:
Finishing Line Press
PO Box 1626
Georgetown, Kentucky 40324
USA

Table of Contents

gibbon 1

otter 3

tiger 5

snake 7

swan 9

rhinoceros 11

porcupine 13

red panda 15

lion 17

owl 19

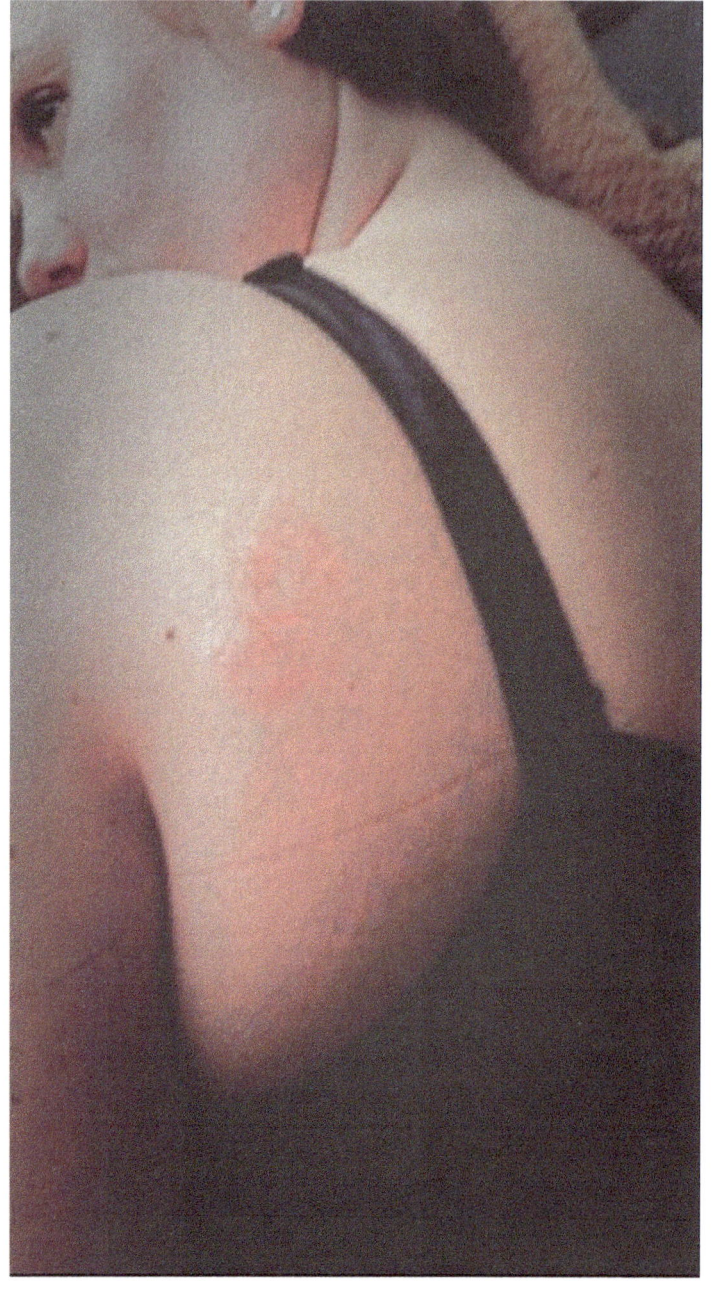

Gibbon

I was too close.

the mother gibbon, a tan all-arms primate, jumped down from above. she *whooped* and *whoo-ed*, a pinch from my face, choral and hot breathed. when I did not retreat, she ripped the flesh from my shoulder with her vampire bat teeth. hallow, she hung in triumph with my blood painted cross'd her lips, the baby cleft onto her shoulder. the infant's aloof mien, and mother's insistent *whoo*, walled the separation between worlds. and yet, I understood the need to guard one's own to my very marrow.

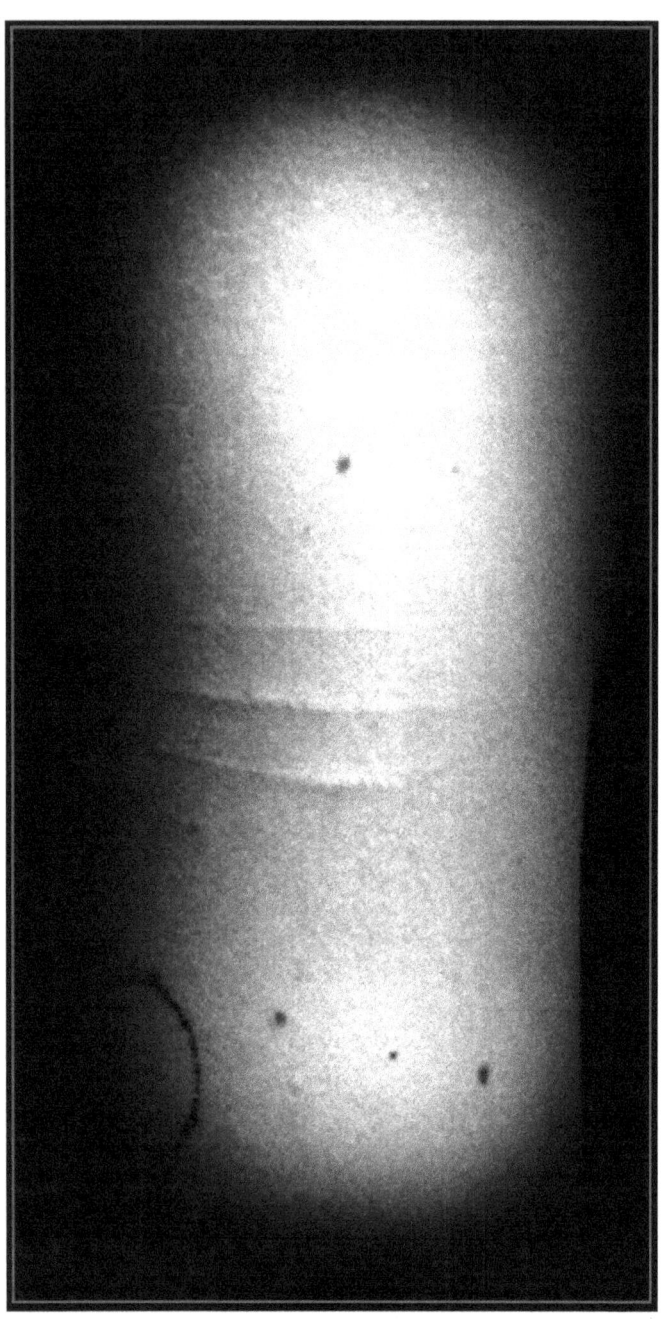

Otter

I imagined myself solid seaside scenery, for he was as belly-full & calm as an otter could be. I wondered: *had he forged for food? eaten kelp? a clam?* webbed feet expanded & he propelled himself off my arm. I was a rock or shore. he circled on his back, ripping loops, until he was a node in the distance. I lifted my body out of the brine & the air stung cold against my arm; three scratches perfectly etched, disinfected by sea salt, lined white across my bicep. when I looked back, the node had vanished, my wound the only proof of his existence.

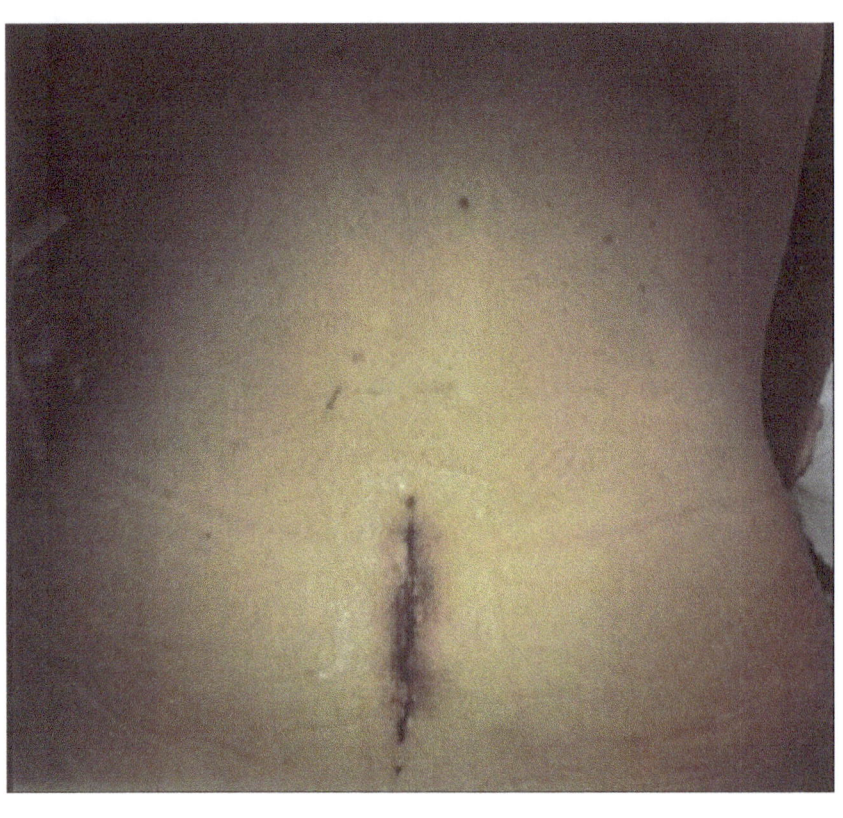

Tiger

the tigress's tail floated erect, its tip submitted—lax, inquisitive. stolid chartreuse eyes locked with mine, their intent lofted parallel to movement. through the steam bath of hot breath, she proposed to unzip me; "that skin suit must be restricting." I drew my hair back from my shoulder & tendered my bare spine, much obliged.

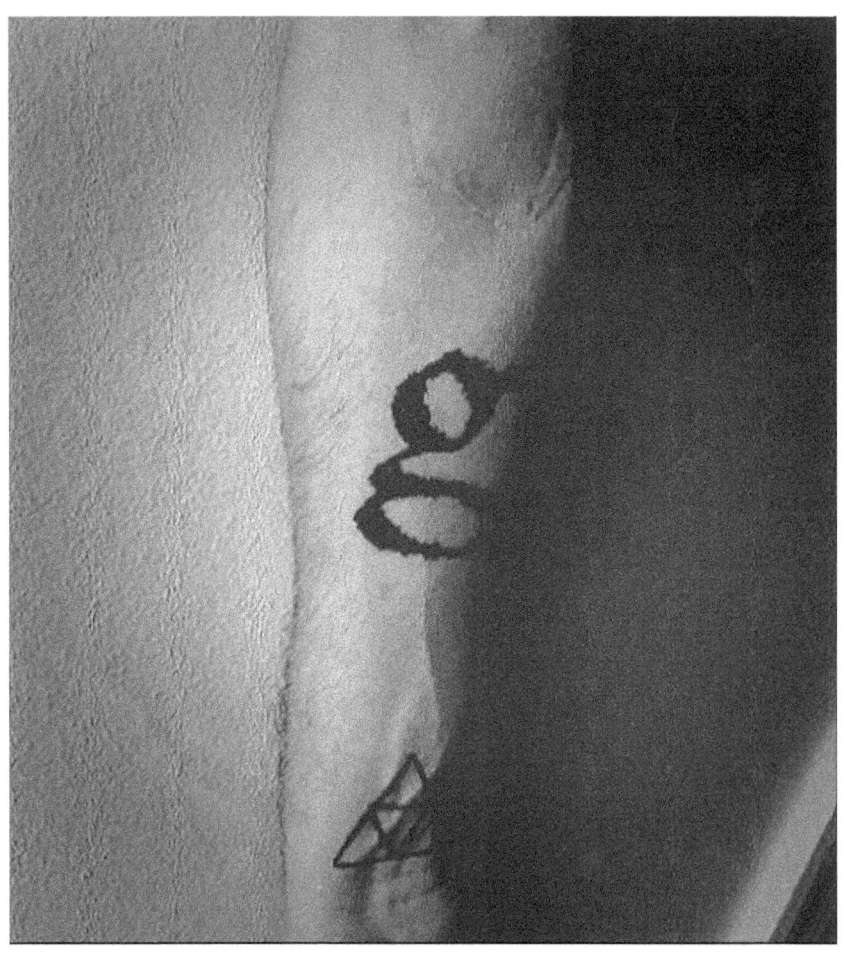

Snake

I underestimated the breadth of my reaction. thunder & strike, I slashed the snake in half. it cringed & writhed, silent. the movement allowed time for my horror to catch up with my spine, quiver & recalibrate. in the soft space between forearm & bicep, serpent fangs had formed a grooved semi-circle, linked top-to-bottom in sanguine. I turned & felt the warm heave of stomach reach my dry throat.

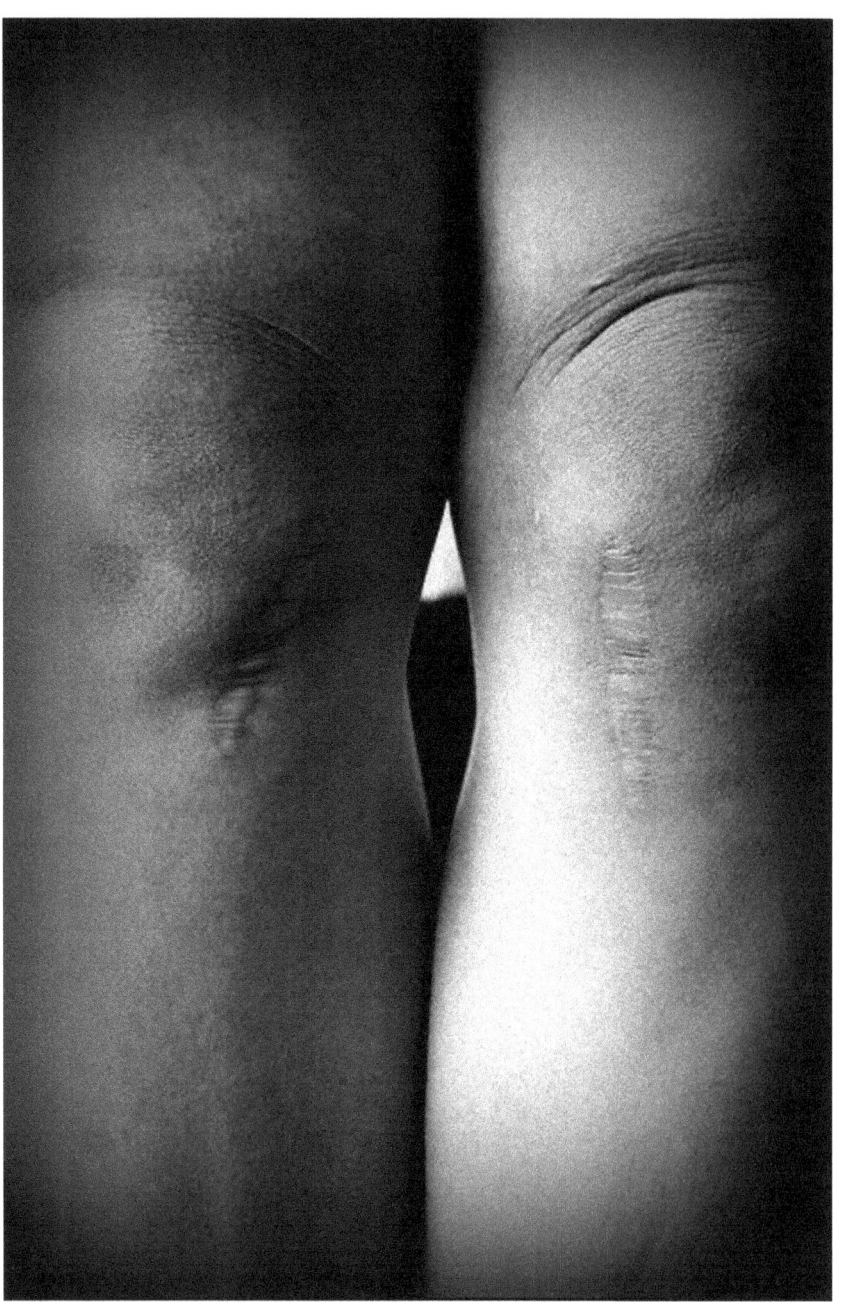

Swan

purple twilight & sleepy fog hugged the edges of the pond. humidity locked my body slow, trapped by the strength & regality of the swan. she exited as direct, unbridled, as her entrance: neck a steel tire iron, and body the fulcrum. the damp grass had padded my collapse; my knees had buckled for the only Queen.

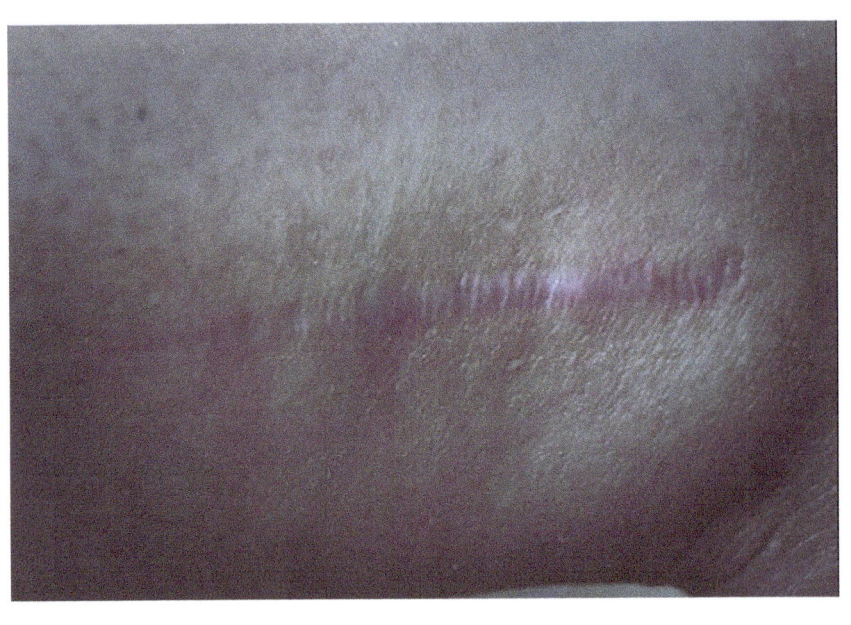

Rhinoceros

the rhino encroached from behind, his skin the terrain of hot sun & impenetrable girth. "Do you take me for a fool?" he asked. "I did not come here to be your clown, your riding horse."
I froze as impala, deer, or elk would, incapable of speech or presence. he penetrated his horn into my ankle, carving a line deep into my skin. I went limp to the ground, akimbo, rag-doll.
he hovered over me, his spears pointed at my brow. he said, "Give me back the horns of my ancestors & I'll cease to haunt you."

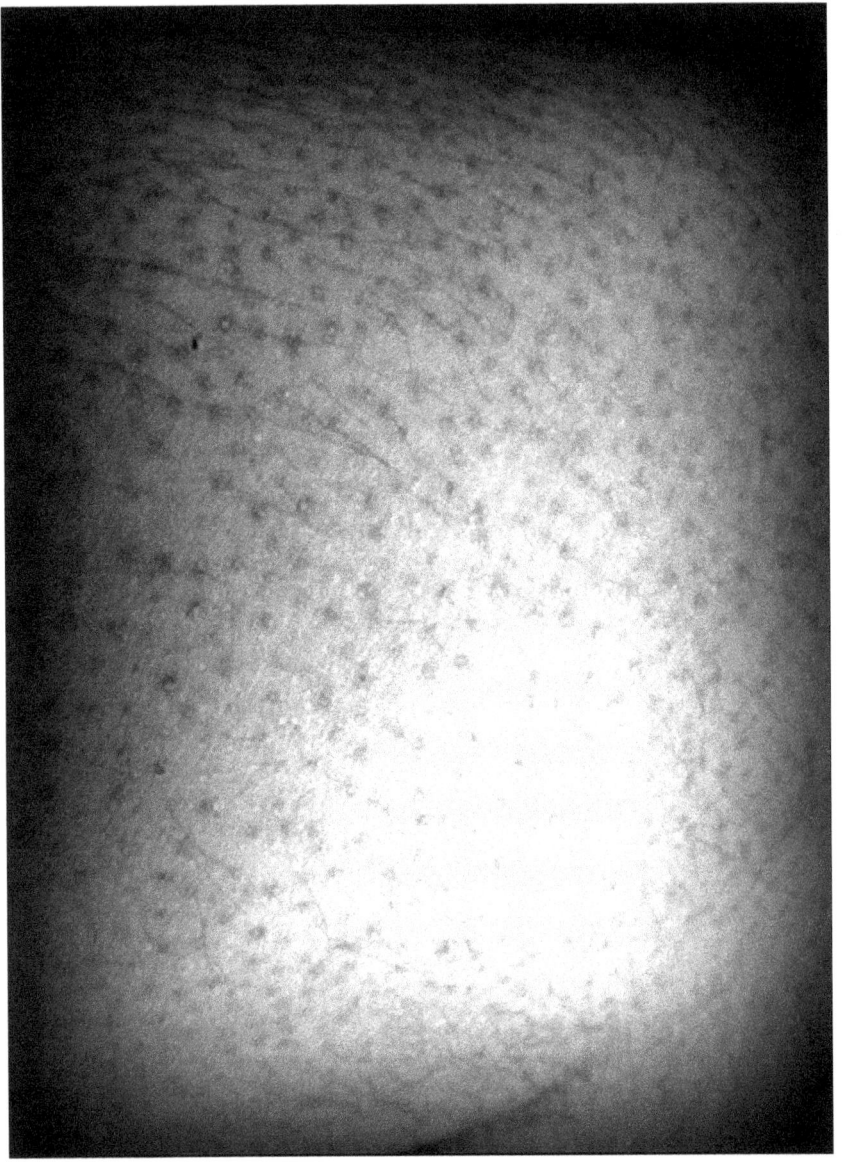

Porcupine

"I thought it was a rock!" he groaned, eyes fixed up to the sky.

I hesitated to yank the quills out in haste or in slow motion, so I plucked the tough spikes from his leg in rhythm. (*pluck*) one by (*pluck*) one, by (*pluck*) one. each (*pluck*) time he squeezed his eyes shut (*pluck*)& clenched the muscles (*pluck*) protecting his femur.

(*pluck*)"I told you to bring your glasses."

(*pluck*) "The porcupine didn't run away," he told me, "it stayed put and I could see it shake, trying to sink into the ground."

(*pluck*) "Defense is defense."

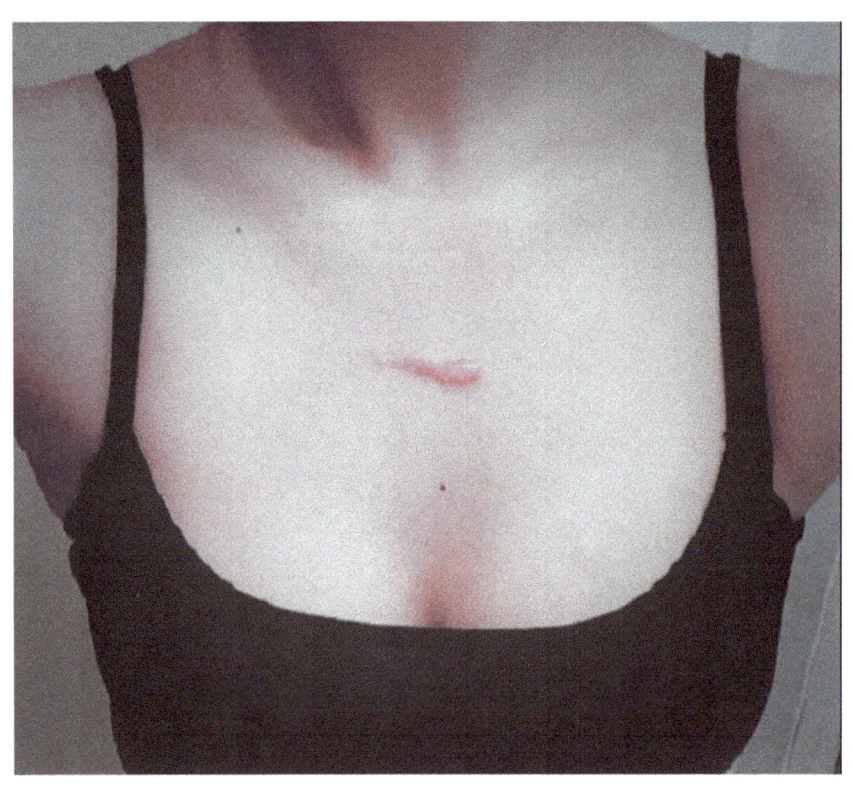

Red Panda

the red panda levered his ringed tail to balance, leapt down branch by branch. he steadied himself upon the lowest bough & sprung into my arms. his white & red bandit face sniffed mine, nose to nose. I felt the numbing needles of anxiety; the sensation muffled how deep his claws burrowed against my chest. more aware than I of our dissemblance, he slowly ascended the tree again, only pausing for seconds to scrutinize the damage he had done. I observed his nose crinkle, bollixed by his handiwork.

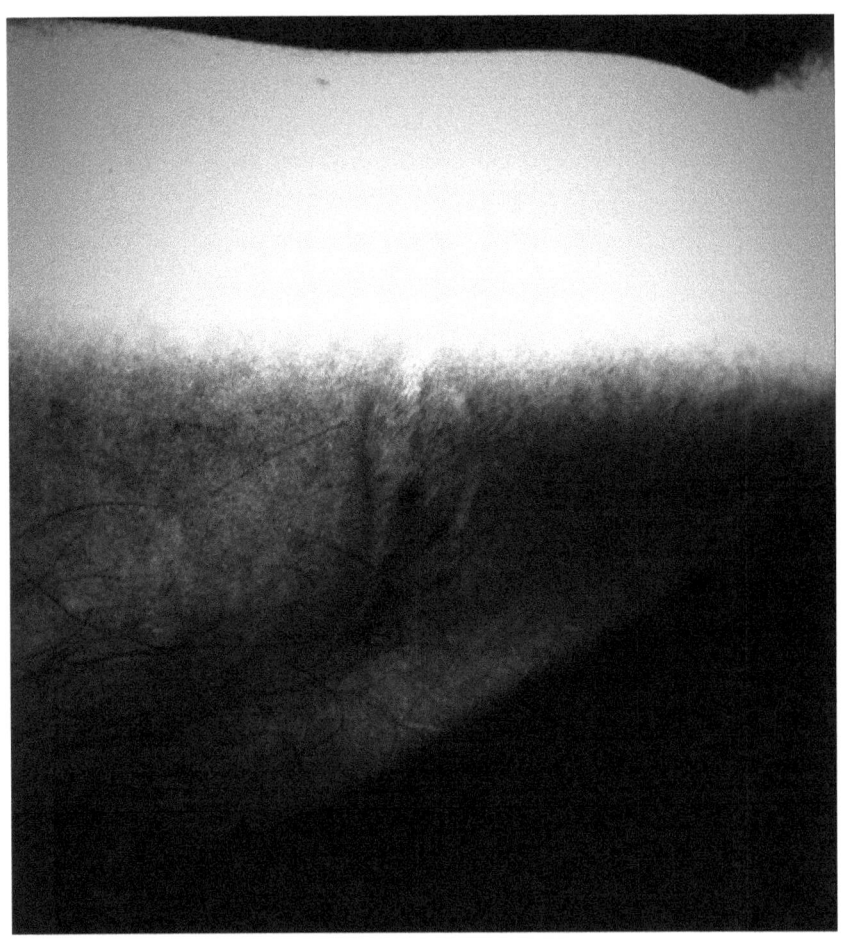

Lion

all day long, the lion paced to and fro, scorched by indefatigable intensity.

"He is grieving," my supervisor said, "looking for his mate."

upon evening, I leaned forward to feed him ribeye from the large metal bowl. the eyes coming toward me warned, "Back away," but duty steadied the offering. impatient, he swiped at the receptacle & snagged his claw on my arm. I held the bloody scratch with my hand, stomping out pain & cursing on the concrete ground. he made his point, the petulant & inconsolable lion, and without remorse, cleaned his supper from the floor.

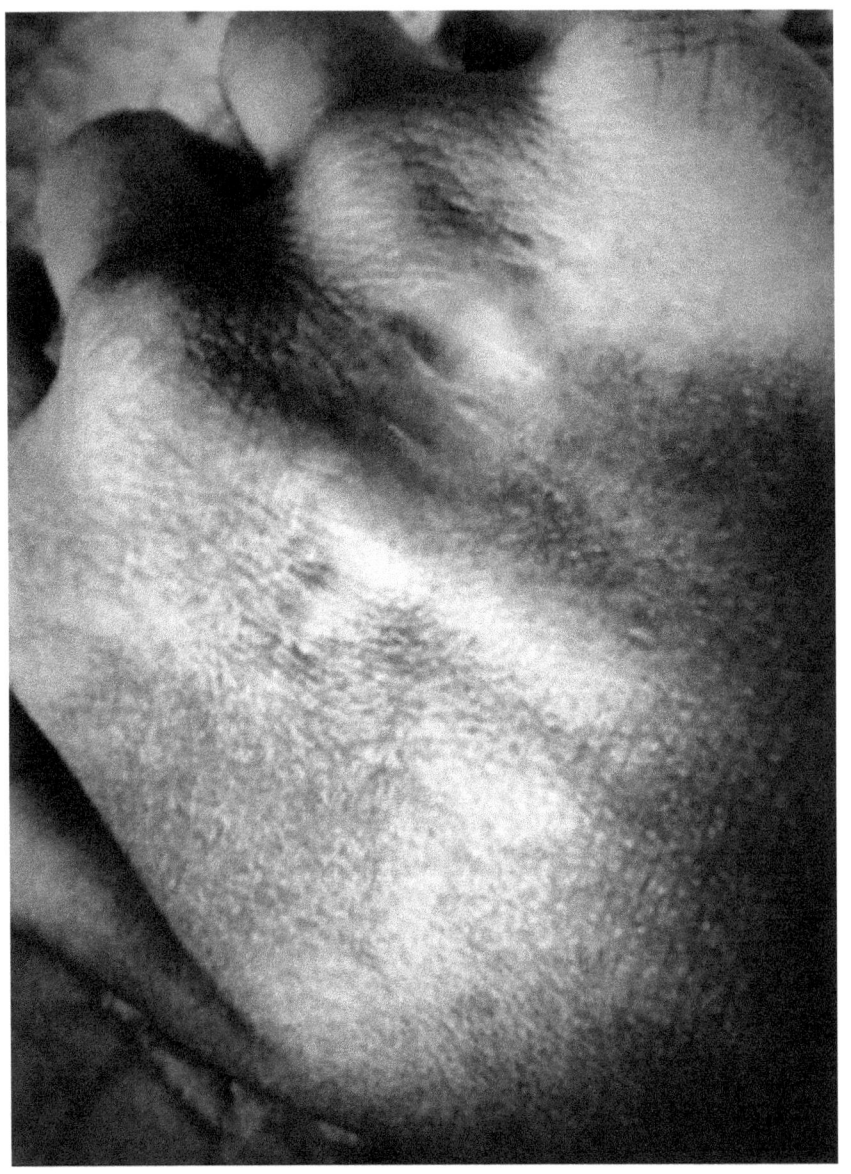

Owl

he sang to me, one summer's eve, of his desire to balance on bare skin & bone. I placed my gloves on the dirt & held my hand out. he mounted, digging in his talons (*push plush prick*). there were many tales he had to tell me: infra-red. mouse squeaks. howling wolves. silence before dawn. the burrow & *coo* of sleep. a recitation of cicadas & the sporadic june bug rustled through his feathers. the sunset smelled of lilac & wood.
"The secret," he *hoo*-ed, "is to trust your ear.
    When you betray your body, all effort fails."

Maggie Hellwig is an educator and writer currently living in Chapel Hill, North Carolina. She received her MFA in Writing from School of the Art Institute of Chicago in 2015 and her BFA in English Literature from Dickinson College in 2007. Her publication record encompasses poetry, fiction, and journalism alike. Her poetry and fiction have been published by *The Atticus Review, Fairlight Books*, and *Curbside Splendor*. She has also written book reviews and editorials for *Chicagoist.com* and *Muftah.org*. She is currently an instructor of English at Northwestern State University of Louisiana and Durham Technical Community College. Her prized possessions include a shy tortoiseshell cat named Emmie Lou, a hefty inventory of books, and an orchid.

www.ingramcontent.com/pod-product-compliance
Lightning Source LLC
Chambersburg PA
CBHW050822090426
42737CB00022B/3477